T0304371

THE LIFE-CHANGING MAGIC OF
DRUMMING

A
**BEGINNER'S
GUIDE**
BY MUSICIAN
NANDI BUSHELL

NANDI BUSHELL

MAGIC CAT 🐾🎵 PUBLISHING

NEW YORK

HI, I'M NANDI BUSHELL.

I'm here to tell you about how drumming
changed my life . . . and share the magic
of drumming with you too.

I STARTED DRUMMING WHEN I WAS FIVE YEARS OLD.

Dad was making us pancakes one weekend, and I was watching Ringo Starr play "Hey Jude." Ringo had a huge smile on his face. I wanted to try it out!

I did well on a math test, so my mom and dad took me to a toy store to celebrate. I chose a small drum kit with two toms.

When we got home I couldn't stop playing the kit . . .

. . . and soon enough I broke through it!

But playing still felt special, new, and exciting. So, I desperately wanted a new kit.

I'm going to be talking about drums a lot, so let's take a look at the **kit** I use. Each part of the kit has a different sound and purpose.

NOTE ON GRIP:

There are two main ways to hold the sticks. **Traditional** grip is when you hold the stick in your left hand between your thumb and forefinger, like this. It's how most jazz drummers play.

Traditional grip

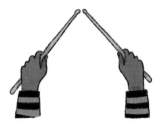

Matched grip

I know how to play traditional grip, but mostly I play **matched**, holding both the sticks the same way.

On either side, the **CRASH CYMBAL** can be used at the start of each bar, to make a loud noise or for texture.

The **HI-HAT** is a type of cymbal you can open and close with your foot pedal or hit with a stick

The **SNARE** makes a sharp sound, almost like a crack

BASS
This has a low, deep sound. You hit it using a foot pedal.

Turn to page 32 for more information on how to hold your sticks!

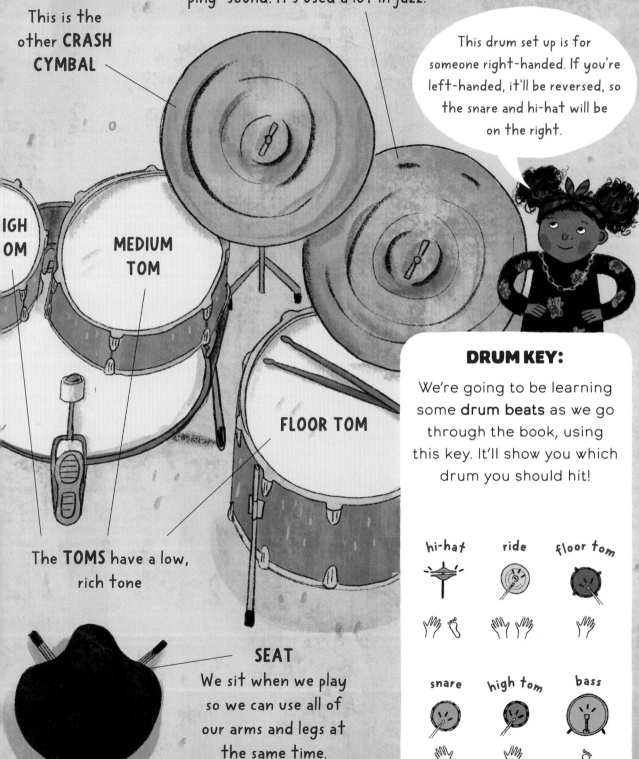

The **RIDE CYMBAL** is on the right. It's a bit quieter than a crash and makes a high "ping" sound. It's used a lot in jazz.

This is the other **CRASH CYMBAL**

This drum set up is for someone right-handed. If you're left-handed, it'll be reversed, so the snare and hi-hat will be on the right.

IGH OM

MEDIUM TOM

FLOOR TOM

The **TOMS** have a low, rich tone

SEAT
We sit when we play so we can use all of our arms and legs at the same time.

DRUM KEY:

We're going to be learning some **drum beats** as we go through the book, using this key. It'll show you which drum you should hit!

hi-hat	ride	floor tom
snare	high tom	bass

MY FIRST REAL DRUM KIT was still quite small. My dad taught me for a bit; then I got a teacher.

I started learning more, and my dad started filming videos of me doing cover songs for fun.

I did a cover of James Brown's "Funky Drummer." Questlove saw it on social media and sent me a bigger drum kit!

When I was nine, Lenny Kravitz heard my cover of Bill Withers, "Use Me," and he started to follow me on Instagram.

I made a cover of his song "Are You Gonna Go My Way." Then he invited me to play at The O2 arena in London! That's when things started blowing up.

During lockdown, I recorded a cover of "Everlong" and sent it to Dave Grohl.

I challenged him to a drum battle, and he said yes! He even wrote a song for me, which was incredible.

Since then, I've played with his band Foo Fighters in front of 20,000 people at the Forum in Los Angeles and 90,000 people at Wembley Stadium in London.

My videos have been watched by millions and millions of viewers. I've also written my own music.

So, let me tell you how I did it, and how you can learn to play the drums like me!

START WITH A BASIC BEAT

Drumming is all about rhythm. I'm going to show you a simple drum beat
I learned when I was starting out.

4/4 is an easy time signature to start with. It's based
on a steady count of 4. Count to 4 in your head.

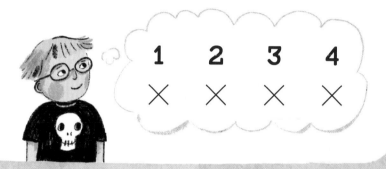

Lots of pop and rock
music is in 4/4 because it's
easy to sing along to. See if
you can count 1, 2, 3, 4 to
your favorite song.

Every time you count,
you hit the hi-hat with
one of your sticks.

See how you're hitting the hi-hat once for every
beat? Those notes are called quarter notes.
Keep your foot pressed down on the pedal
so the hi-hat is closed when you hit it.

Now we're going to
start adding in the
other drum parts.

When drumming, your
hands are often doing
different things than
your legs or feet.

It's like rubbing your
tummy and patting your
head at the same time.

If you can do that, you can learn the drums. It just takes practice.

When you're ready, you hit the snare with your other stick on beats 2 and 4.

If you've got that, then add the bass on beats 1 and 3.

You've just learned a standard **backbeat**!

A backbeat means the stronger sound is on beats 2 and 4.

DON'T BE AFRAID TO TRY SOMETHING NEW

A **fill** is the magic that helps you change from one beat to another.

If you're playing a standard backbeat, like the one you just learned, a fill can help you go from a verse to a chorus.

Fills are also cool because you can experiment with them and even do a drum solo.

When I was 5, my dad taught me my first fill. He's not a drummer, so he learned it from an online tutorial. It's called . . .

. . . Splat Boom Deb-bie Boom!

It's called that because that's the sound the drums make when you play it!

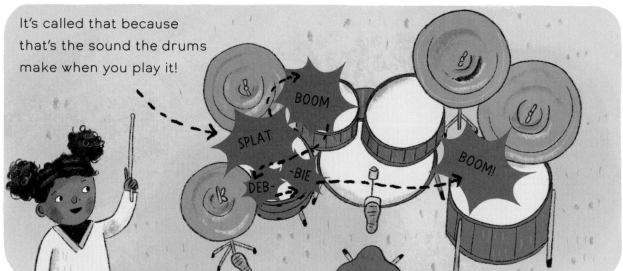

Start by counting to 4 in your head again, like you did for the standard backbeat. But this time, put an "and" after the number 3.

On count 1, hit the snare. Then on two, hit the high tom.

	1	2	3	AND	4
🥁		×			
🥁	×				

On count 3 and the "and" after, hit the snare. Do you see how you're hitting it twice as fast as before? These shorter notes are called **eighth notes**. Finally, hit the floor tom on beat 4.

	1	2	3	AND	4
🥁		×			
🥁	×		×	×	
🥁					×

It goes snare, tom, snare-snare, tom. Splat, Boom, Deb-bie, Boom!

Once you've got this, you can experiment a bit by adding different parts of the kit. Don't be afraid to try something new!

LOOK AFTER YOURSELF . . . AND YOUR NEIGHBORS!

Drumming is very physical.

When you're really feeling the music, you might hit the drums pretty hard. When I play a drum roll, I'm in the moment and I'm one with the drum kit. It's really exciting.

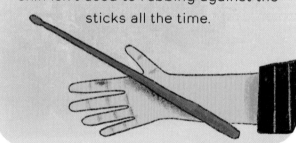

When you're learning, you can get blisters on your hands because your skin isn't used to rubbing against the sticks all the time.

I used to get blisters on my feet from the double pedals too.

I don't get them as often now because my hands and feet are stronger.

If you get a blister, put a bandage on it and stop playing if it's too uncomfortable.

It's very important to wear ear protection when you're drumming.

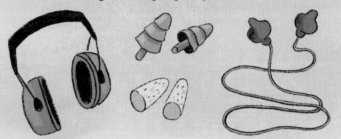

Use ear plugs or noise isolation headphones. If you don't, you might get tinnitus, which can cause buzzing or ringing in your ear all the time.

I used to have these big purple headphones that were pretty aesthetic with my look.

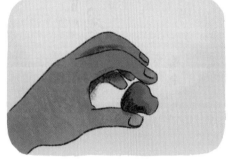

Now I get plugs fitted for my ears.

You've got to be considerate of people around you. I have an electric drum kit that you can't hear outside.

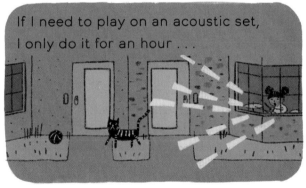

If I need to play on an acoustic set, I only do it for an hour . . .

. . . and never after 7 o'clock in the evening.

#4 BOTH HANDS ARE IMPORTANT

It doesn't matter if you're right- or left-handed: for drumming you need to build up the strength in both of your hands and wrists.

Drummers practice **rudiments**, which are small patterns, to build up speed and technique.

The simplest rudiment is **single strokes**.

Tap the snare drum first with your right stick . . .

then your left.

It's as simple as **R L R L**.

Then tap your right again, then left. Right, left, right, left.

You start it slowly at first, then speed up!

The next rudiment is **double strokes**.

It's very similar, but you tap twice.

It goes right-right . . .

left-left.
R R L L R R L L.

Then, try hitting triples, so three strokes in a row.

Right-right-right,
left-left-left,
RRRLLL
RRRLLL.

You can use a single, double or a triple stroke for a drum roll!

A **paradiddle** is a great way of changing which hand leads on a beat. Just remember you change hands between "pa" and "ra," then hit "did" and "dle" with the same hand. So it's R L R R L R L L . . .

Right — Pa-

Left — ra-

Right — did-

Right — dle

Left — Pa-

Right — ra-

Left — did-

Left — dle

See how your starting hand changes each paradiddle? It's a nifty trick!

Now try starting with your weaker hand, so if you're right-handed, start with your left!

#5   MAKE TIME FOR OTHER INTERESTS

Drums aren't the only instrument I play.

I love playing jazz on the saxophone.

As with drums (and every instrument), you need rhythm to play the sax . . .

but it's a different technique because you make sounds by putting your tongue on the reed and blowing.

I also play piano, which I find quite difficult. Your hands have to do different things: One might be playing single notes while the other might be playing chords made up of several notes at the same time.

I like to play my favorite rock songs on guitar and bass guitar too.

And for my 13th birthday I asked for a flute. I really love learning to play it.

It gets easier to learn other instruments when you've already learned one!

There are also so many different types of drums—not just drum kits!
Countries around the world have their own drums and styles of playing them.

The **steelpan** is a tuned drum played in Caribbean steelbands. It can have up to 30 different notes!

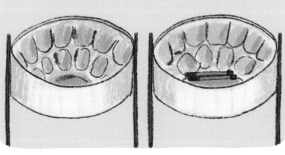

A **djembe** drum is West African. You play it with your bare hands, and it can make low-, medium-, and high-pitched sounds.

And big drums called **surdos** are played in Brazilian samba bands.

You'll be surprised by how much cool music is out there!
Watching different types of bands is so inspiring.

I work really hard, but I know it's important to take time for yourself.

I love to draw, paint, or play games with my brother.

I also have a half-pipe in my backyard. However you relax, make sure you make time to do it!

#6 FIND YOUR OWN STYLE

There are so many ways to play drums—everyone has their own unique style.

Rock drummers play really hard, and it's exciting to hear.

Heavy metal drummers often play with double pedals, which sound fast and satisfying.

My style is very open. I love heavy metal and rock, but I love jazz, funk, and breakbeats too.

Try different things and find what you love to play.

Here's another drum beat you can try when you're starting out. You'll hear it in lots of different rock songs. It's the same time signature as we've done before, to a beat of 4.

Count to 4 in your head, putting an "and" in between each number:

1 AND **2** AND **3** AND **4** AND

Every time you say either a number or an "and," hit the hi-hat.

1   AND   2   AND   3   AND   4   AND

X   X   X   X   X   X   X   X

Do you see how we're hitting the hi-hat two times for every beat? These shorter notes are eighth notes. You tried them before in the fill on page 11.

Then, add the snare on notes 2 and 4. When you're comfortable with that, the next thing to add is the bass drum on notes 1 and 3.

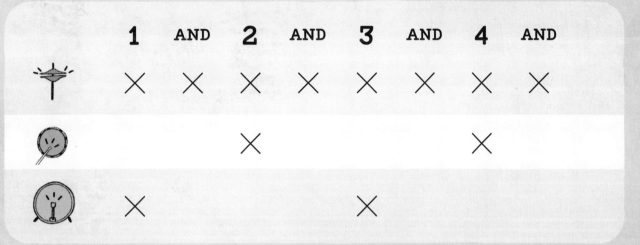

	1	AND	2	AND	3	AND	4	AND
hi-hat	X	X	X	X	X	X	X	X
snare			X				X	
bass drum	X				X			

Now it's time to learn how to play an open hi-hat!

An open hi-hat is played by lifting your foot off the pedal. Do this on beat 1,

then close it on the "and" by pressing your foot down on the pedal.

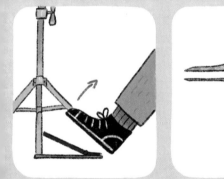   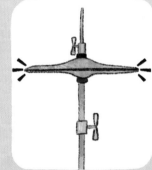

While you're doing this, keep playing the hi-hat with your stick too, as you've been doing on page 18. Notice how the hi-hat symbol has a circle above the x on the 1? That's where you open the hi-hat. The plus sign is where you close it.

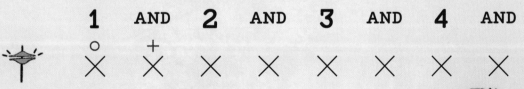

	1	AND	2	AND	3	AND	4	AND
hi-hat	o X	+ X	X	X	X	X	X	X

The sound an open hi-hat makes is called a sizzle!

You've got it!

MUSIC ISN'T A COMPETITION

Sometimes I play in competitions at school.

I won on saxophone . . .

and the advanced percussion.

It's fun when you win . . .

. . .but when you don't win you feel disappointed.

I think music is so hard to judge, especially if there are different instruments in the competition. They're all amazing to hear.

So if you enter something and you don't win, don't worry about it! You should make music because it's fun and not because you want to win.

And it's fun to play **with** people, not against them!

At school, I play in the orchestra.

That gives me the chance to play the timpani and other cool percussive instruments!

Timpani   Bass Drum   Snare Drum   Xylophone   Gong   Triangle   Cymbals

My family and I always say that music is art. If you've made people feel something through your music, you've won.

PRACTICE, PRACTICE, PRACTICE!

I didn't just get the coordination to play drums within a month or so.
I've been playing for more than eight years.

To play drums,
you need to practice,

practice,

practice!

SUMMER CONCERT

I'm a perfectionist, so I like getting things right—but it can be fun when it goes wrong.
Sometimes you just have to try again, and again, and again!

"Caravan," a jazz classic, was the hardest
song I've learned. It took me three months!

I never felt like giving up.
Even though it was difficult,
it was thrilling to play.

Jazz sounds different
because the main
part of a jazz beat
is a triplet pattern,
which means three
notes are played for
every beat.

Rock has a straighter rhythm while jazz is bouncier.
We call this bouncy rhythm **swing**.

Here's a simple jazz groove you can play.

Start by counting to 4 in your head like we've been doing. Every time you say a number, hit the ride cymbal with your right hand.

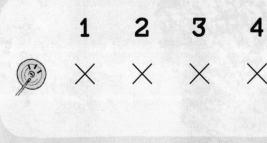

	1	2	3	4
	X	X	X	X

Then add hi-hat pedal strokes by tapping your left foot on the hi-hat pedal on beats 2 and 4.

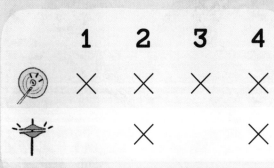

	1	2	3	4
(ride)	X	X	X	X
(hi-hat)		X		X

Jazz beats work in triplets, which means you divide each beat into three. So it's:

1	AND	UH	2	AND	UH	3	AND	UH	4	AND	UH

We're going to play a **swing pattern**, adding the ride cymbal on the "uh" of beats 2 and 4.

	1	AND	UH	2	AND	UH	3	AND	UH	4	AND	UH
(ride)	X			X			X		X		X		X

Now let's play the ride cymbal swing pattern and your hi-hat pedal strokes together!

	1	AND	UH	2	AND	UH	3	AND	UH	4	AND	UH
(ride)	X			X			X		X		X		X
(hi-hat)				X						X		

DON'T BE AFRAID TO ASK FOR WHAT YOU WANT

When I was 10, I challenged Dave Grohl to a drum battle during lockdown.

I never thought he'd respond. But he saw my cover of "Everlong," and he said yes!

He came back with "Dead End Friends" by Them Crooked Vultures.

That song wasn't too hard for me. I just had to practice.

I sent him my version . . .

It was heating up.

His next move was to write a song about me, which is just called "Nandi." Isn't that mind-blowing?!

So then I wrote a song about him, called "Rock and Grohl."

Eventually, he admitted defeat on a talk show.

A year later, I was in the United States with my family and Foo Fighters were playing at the Forum in Los Angeles. I wanted to play with them!

My Dad emailed Dave's management to ask him if I could jam, and he said:

FROM: Dave Grohl
TO : Nandi

THAT WOULD BE AWESOME !!!

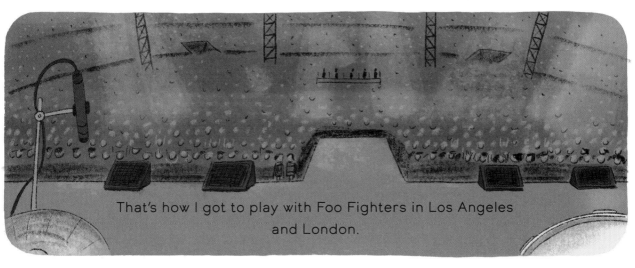

That's how I got to play with Foo Fighters in Los Angeles and London.

It just shows that if you want something, you should ask for it.

You never know what might happen. I love to collaborate with people. It makes my music stronger.

It adds a new depth to a song you might not have had on your own.

#10 EXPRESS YOURSELF

I love that I can express myself through drumming. I can let it all out.

If I'm having a hard day at school or just need some "me" time, I always turn to the drum kit.

Everything about it makes me light up with joy!

Sometimes I go to jam nights.

Musicians bring their instruments but no one has rehearsed the song.

It starts with a guitar riff and everyone will make up something to go with it.

You've got to listen to each other really carefully while you play to make sure you're all together.

It's so cool because you come up with something totally new every time. It's called **improvisation**, and I love it.

I can also express myself through writing my own music.

I get inspiration from lots of different places.

When I was 11, I wrote a song called "The Shadows" for my dad after he went through depression.

That's the amazing thing about music—something sad can inspire your art.

It can help you come to terms with things in your life and make challenges seem easier to tackle.

AND REMEMBER . . . NEVER STOP AIMING FOR THE STARS!

Drumming can be hard work sometimes. However, you must keep going and always have fun. You never know what you might achieve.

There's still so much I want to do.

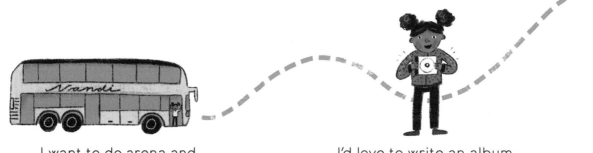

I want to do arena and stadium tours.

I'd love to write an album.

I love to write my own music. Here's how I do it.

1

When I'm writing songs, I get a riff down first on either the piano or the guitar.

2

Next, I get the backbeat with a simple drum beat.

3

Then I create the structure (so, splitting it into verses and choruses) . . .

More than anything, I want to make the world a better place through music.

Hopefully I'll win Grammys. (Although winning is not important, they would look pretty cool on display in my house).

I also want to write music for movies. And of course have fun!

4

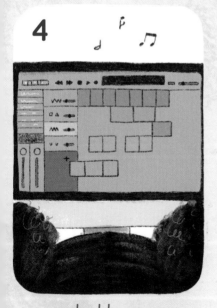

...and add some more instruments, like synths, and make the drums a bit more interesting.

The lyrics come last, for me.

The most important thing for me is to write music from my heart.

Here's a simple song structure I like to use:

A Verse
B Chorus
A Verse
B Chorus
C Bridge
B Chorus

It's the most common way to write a pop or rock song!

BEFORE I GO,

Drumming has changed my life in so many ways. If you're just starting out, then the best advice I can give to you is to just have fun.

Practice, practice, practice and ROCK OUT!!!
If you're enjoying it, people can tell.

Don't be afraid to try new things and ask for what you want.

Make time to play with other people.
I've learned so much that way and
made great friends too.

HOW TO . . . DO A DRUM ROLL!

I love drum rolls. When I do them, I'm really at one with the music and in the moment. There are many different ways you can do them, but this is a good place to start.

1

 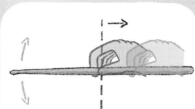

First, make sure you're holding your drum sticks in the right place. One at a time, hold your sticks between your thumb and finger.

Aim for the middle, then move your hand down 3 finger widths.

This is the perfect gripping point, as you'll get the most bounce.

2 Start with your single stroke rudiment, which we practiced on page 14. Hit right, then left, then right, then left. Gradually build up speed until it becomes a roll, but make sure you're keeping the strokes even.

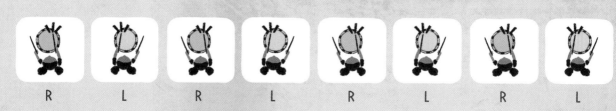

R   L   R   L   R   L   R   L

When you're ready, you can try your double stroke rudiment. Hit right, right, left, left, right, right, left, left.

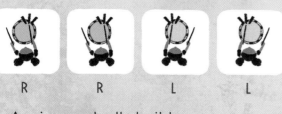

R   R   L   L

Again, gradually build up your speed until it becomes a roll.

Well done! And try not to hold your drumsticks too tightly— you want to make sure they can bounce.

HOW TO . . . PLAY "FUNKY DRUMMER"

You might recognize this beat from James Brown's **"Funky Drummer."** It's the most sampled beat in the history of hip-hop and it's a must-learn! To play it, you need to first learn how to play **sixteenth notes**.

1 Count to 4 again in your head.

1	2	3	4
X	X	X	X

Sixteenth notes break up the beat into 4 notes. So you're hitting twice as fast as eighth notes. It might be helpful to add "e-and-uh" between the beats in your head. Try this beat on the hi-hat, using your right hand only. You might need to practice this one to get up speed!

2

1 E AND UH **2** E AND UH **3** E AND UH **4** E AND UH

X X X X X X X X X X X X X X X X

Once you've got that, try adding the snare on beats 2 and 4. Hit it with your left hand as your right hand is busy hitting the hi-hat sixteenth notes.

3

1 E AND UH **2** E AND UH **3** E AND UH **4** E AND UH

X X X X X X X X X X X X X X X X

           X   X

Then, when you're comfortable with the first three steps, it's time to add the bass drum. Start by adding it just on the 1. Then add it on the "and" of both 1 and 3 and the "e" of 4.

	1	E	AND	UH	2	E	AND	UH	3	E	AND	UH	4	E	AND	UH
hi-hat	X	X	X	X	X	X	X	X	X	X	X	X	X	X	X	X
snare					X								X			
bass drum	X		X						X		X			X		

Now we'll add some ghost notes—you play these softer than normal notes—on the snare, on the "uh" of 2, the "e" of 3 and the "uh" of 4.

	1	E	AND	UH	2	E	AND	UH	3	E	AND	UH	4	E	AND	UH
hi-hat	X	X	X	X	X	X	X	X	X	X	X	X	X	X	X	X
snare					X			×		×			X			×
bass drum	X		X						X		X			X		

Now it's time for something tricky.

You're going to add another ghost note on the "uh" of 3, just before hitting a normal note on the snare for beat 4. That means you're hitting a soft note then a hard note right afterward. This is challenging to do but keep practicing! If you can do this then you can do ANYTHING!

Then, finally, if you're OK with all of this (you're doing really well!) you can start adding open hi-hats. Try opening the hi-hat on the "e" of beats 2 and 4. See how this changes the sound?

This is a challenging groove to play. Remember, you can always slow it down while you're learning, then bring it up to speed when you're confident.

ALL ABOUT NANDI

Nandi was born in Durban, South Africa, on April 28, 2010. She moved with her family to the United Kingdom when she was two years old.

Nandi, age 11, with her family

Nandi began drumming when she was five and started taking lessons at age six. With her dad's help, she began posting videos of her covers of different songs online. Her drum cover of Nirvana's "In Bloom" went viral in November 2019, gaining 10 million views within a week.

During the Covid-19 pandemic, Nandi uploaded a cover of "Everlong" by Foo Fighters and challenged drummer Dave Grohl to a drum-off. The battle drew millions of views and made Nandi a household name. Nandi has since performed with Foo Fighters at the Forum in Los Angeles and Wembley Stadium in London.

Nandi playing her first (toy) drum kit, age 5

Nandi, age 9, with Questlove at Blackheath Festival

Nandi, age 11, on stage at The Forum in LA with Foo Fighters

Nandi, age 9, on the set of a John Lewis department store ad

Nandi also plays lead and bass guitar and writes her own music. With Roman Morello, she wrote and performed "The Children Will Rise Up" in October 2021 to warn of the dangers of climate change. President Barack Obama used the piece at the 2021 United Nations Climate Change Conference.

In 2021, Cartoon Network named Nandi their first musician-in-residence. In 2023, she completed her first speaking acting role, performing as Emerald, the goddaughter of Brian May (The Godfather of Rock) in the Children's BBC TV series *Andy and the Band*.

Nandi performing at the Platinum Jubilee in front of Buckingham Palace, age 12

Nandi playing with Young Voices, age 13

In 2024, she toured with Young Voices, the world's largest children's choir, as a star guest artist, performing live to over 600,000 people. Nandi's dream is to be the best musician she can be and have as much fun as possible along the way.

GLOSSARY

Acoustic: an instrument that is not made louder by electrical equipment

Bar: a small section of music that holds the same number of beats as the time signature.

Beat: the steady pulse you feel when listening to a piece of music. The beat is what you would naturally clap along to.

Breakbeat: a kind of drum pattern that is repeated in hip-hop and dance music

Bridge: a change in melody that provides variety and connects two sections of a song

Cover: a new version of an existing song

Cymbal: a brass plate you strike with a stick to make a sound

Eighth note: a note that lasts for half a beat. In a 4/4 time signature, you would play 8 eighth notes in a bar.

Ghost notes: very quiet hits on a drum, usually the snare

Lyrics: the words in a song

Orchestra: a group of musicians playing instruments together

Percussion: musical instruments that are played by hitting them

Quarter note: a note that lasts for one beat. One quarter note lasts for as long as two eighth notes. In a 4/4 time signature, you would play 4 quarter notes in a bar.

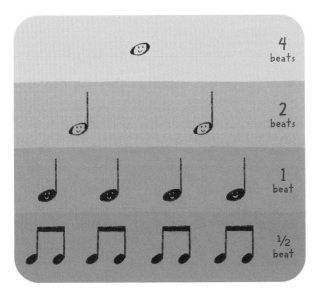

Riff: a short, often catchy music pattern that is repeated again and again

Rhythm: a regular pattern of different sounds, some long and some short

Sixteenth note: a note lasting for a quarter of a beat. In a 4/4 time signature, you would play 16 in a bar.

Swing: a style of jazz music popular in the 1930s

Synths: short for *synthesizer*, which is an electronic instrument that produces a range of recorded sounds

Texture: the effect of different layers of sound in a piece of music

Time signature: in music, the structure that tells you how many beats there are in a bar.

Verse: the section of a song that normally features different lyrics each time it's repeated

I dedicate this book to all the people, girls and boys, young and old, who never got the opportunity
to learn to play the drums and wanted to. You are never too young or too old to enjoy
the life-changing magic of playing the drums.

I want to thank my family, Dave Grohl, Lenny Kravitz, Questlove, Tom Morello, all my teachers,
and everyone who has ever supported and believed in me. Without all the love, support, encouragement,
and opportunities, I would not have experienced all that I have so far. Thank you.

Thank you, James Brown, for reviewing all the lessons in my book.

NB

For my husband, who is my favorite rock star,
and for all the kids who love music.

AS

The illustrations in this book were created digitally.
Set in Calder and Vodka Sans.

ISBN 978-1-4197-7608-3

Text © 2024 Nandi Bushell
Illustrations © 2024 Andrea Stegmaier
Cover © 2024 Magic Cat
Book design by Stephanie Jones
Fact-checking and editorial assistance by Keiran Pearson

First published in the North America in 2024 by Magic Cat Publishing,
an imprint of ABRAMS. First published in the United Kingdom in 2024 by
Magic Cat Publishing Ltd.

Printed and bound in China
10 9 8 7 6 5 4 3 2 1

Abrams books are available at special discounts when purchased in quantity
for premiums and promotions as well as fundraising or educational use
Special editions can also be created to specification. For details, contact
specialsales@abramsbooks.com or the address below.

MIX
Paper | Supporting
responsible forestry
FSC® C144853

FURTHER READING

**Music and How It Works: The Complete Guide
for Kids,** by DK

Rebel Girls Rock: 25 Tales of Women in Music, by
Rebel Girls, foreword by Joan Jett

**Turn It Up!: A Pitch-Perfect History of Music
That Rocked the World,** by National
Geographic Kids

What Is Rock and Roll? by Jim O'Connor and
Who HQ, illustrated by Gregory Copeland

ABRAMS The Art of Books
195 Broadway, New York, NY 10007
abramsbooks.com

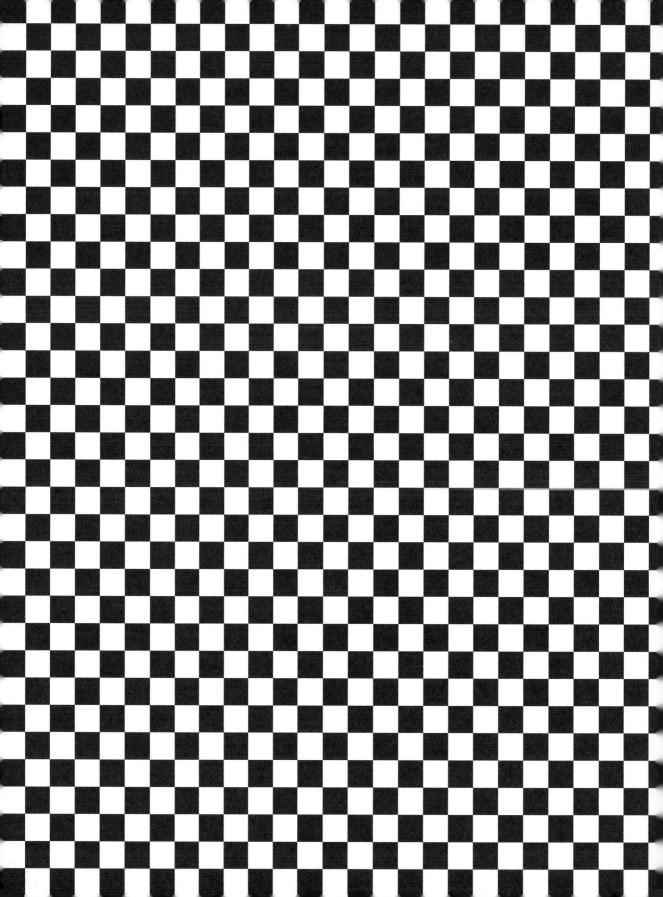